LETTUCE BE THE CHANGE
COOKBOOK

RECIPES USING FRESH PRODUCE FROM AMERICA'S GROWERS

D1609607

*Answering the First Lady's call to end obesity,
one chef and one special school come together
to change the way the American family
eats and cooks!*

Written By Adrienne Saldivar-Meier

Library of Congress Control Number: 2012913101

ISBN-13: 978-0-615-67416-2

Lettuce Be The Change
449 Vista Del Mar Drive
Aptos, CA 95003

Writer: Adrienne Saldivar-Meier

Editor: Lisa Vitarisi Mathews

Designer: Olivia Cajefe Trinidad

Copy Editor: Carrie Gwynne

Photographer: Adrienne Saldivar-Meier

To order visit:
www.lettucebethechange.com

Printed in the United States of America

Lettuce Be the Change recommends that all fruits and vegetables be rinsed or washed before consuming.

CONTENTS

CHAPTER 1
MANN PACKING COMPANY   8

CHAPTER 2
SAGE FRUIT COMPANY   34

ABOUT THE AUTHOR AND PHOTOGRAPHER

Adrienne Saldivar-Meier is a professional Home Cook and Recipe Developer for America's top agricultural growers. She also produces and stars in California's "Simply Fresh" healthy cooking television segments. Adrienne enjoys writing about and photographing food for magazines and cookbooks. She travels all over the United States, conducting healthy-eating cooking demonstrations and presenting fresh produce from national growers.

Adrienne's most rewarding work is providing educational healthy cooking instruction for schools, health institutions, migrant families, and after-school programs. She was invited to the White House to participate in the First Lady's "Chefs Move to Schools" campaign. This cookbook is Adrienne's response to our First Lady's call to action to aid in the fight against childhood obesity.

Adrienne conducts cooking instruction at her coastal home in Monterey Bay, California, and offers cooking retreats at her Pacific Northwest Log lodge outside of Spokane, Washington.

Adrienne is a woman of passion, and that is reflected in her first self-published cookbook.

To purchase additional copies of this book, visit: www.lettucebethechange.com

The website also includes information about Chef Adrienne's cooking classes, cooking retreats, and Chef demonstrations.

IN MEMORY OF MY MOM

Carmen Perez Saldivar
June 7, 1922—May 24, 2011

You cheered the work I do with kids and saw me make it to the White House—I only wish that I could have autographed the first book for you!

You changed the way that I do life. You taught me to make lemonade out of lemons! Because of you, I know what is important. That is why I sit at your kitchen table on this sun-filled morning and write this book for all the moms, dads, and children longing to share a family meal together.

I miss you deeply, Mom, but I am looking forward to sitting at the table that you are preparing for our great reunion!

With love, your daughter,
Adrienne

DEDICATION

To My Husband Mark

You built me the test kitchen of my dreams, the Log Lodge Cooking Retreat, for my passion, and shocked all of us when you went to Italy with me and became the best pasta maker in the class, even when you couldn't boil water back home. You amaze me and I wouldn't be the woman I am without you!

Thank you, Mark. This book is dedicated to you in the same way you have been dedicated to me!

Love,
Adrienne

Adrienne in the White House Garden

be the change™

INTRODUCTION

As a Hispanic youth navigating adolescence, I was reluctant to admit my passion for the kitchen. When school was out during summer, the other kids enjoyed afternoon movie matinees, mixed parties, and shopping mall rendezvous. I was, however, in bliss cutting apricots in one-hundred degree weather in a small orchard in east San Jose, California. As I sliced through the rich orange flesh and flicked the pit into a small, sticky wooden box, my mind would be concocting combinations of ingredients necessary for a new recipe.

Because food brought me so much enjoyment and emotional comfort, my strength also proved to have its down side—I started to get chubby.

I was hurt by the teasing, devastated by the broken dates, and I avoided mirrors! Decades of fad diets controlled my self-esteem or lack of it. I felt that no one understood the shame and self-loathing that I had secretly harbored for over three decades.

My cooking mentor and friend, Chef Paola Baccetti from Italy, ignited my path of change. She took me through the farms of Tuscany and the fields of her own life experience and taught me the power of fresh food and gave me the key to the most important ingredient in world—cooking. She also had no problem sharing her observation of Americans' relationship with cooking. She boldly informed me that we Americans tend to simply "stress our food." Not that we are stressed when we cook, but that we actual put stress into our food with our unconscious attitudes. She recommended that we turn off our cell

Rancho Cielo Culinary Students

phones, TVs, and laptops and pay loving attention to the pot of vegetable soup that we are stirring. It's a crazy yet simple idea and it works! And, as a result of this practice, the most important ingredient that lingers in the food is LOVE, which comes from our now-available hearts. Ironically, this simple truth about being in the present moment taught me to be available to myself and to the community around me.

I recently had the privilege of being invited to the White House and the White House Garden to support our First Lady's national "Chef's Move To Schools" campaign, sponsored by the US Department of Agriculture.

Our First Lady's message was clear and urgent. She asked the 750 chefs from all over the world who were present to commit to making a change in our youths' eating habits. She requested that we each adopt a school to implement food education. Since I was already implementing food education in

Monterey County, California, I decided to challenge my personal commitment and answer the First Lady's call to action with this cookbook.

I chose to adopt the students of Rancho Cielo Youth Campus in Salinas, California. These students are making a difference in their own lives. They are at-risk youth who are each dedicated to changing his or her life path. The students at the Drummond Culinary Academy at Rancho Cielo are creating, tasting, and testing many of my recipes. These Rancho Cielo students are dedicated to passing on the healthy-eating message to their families, their community, and their world at large.

So "Lettuce Be the Change" for a better me, a better us, a better community, and ultimately a better world!

May all your food be filled with love,

Adrienne Salidvar-Meier
Professional Home Cook &
Recipe Developer

MANN PACKING COMPANY

The Mann Packing Family is just that—a real family. And like most families, they are always making up new recipes to share with their loved ones. Daughter Gina, and her chef husband Kevin are passionate about their veggies and it shows by the way they serve their community. Gina has been a part of the non-profit organization Healthy Eating Lifestyle Principles for years. Her dedication to making a healthy change in the American family's diet knows no bounds—she was instrumental in getting me to the White House! Gina's deep caring and passion is evident in the vegetables that her family produces. I love the fact her brother came up with an innovative way to use the very nutritious part of the broccoli stalk by shredding it like a slaw and packaging it for ease. This product alone has changed the way I eat! I use Broccoli Cole Slaw in everything—and I mean everything! Cookies, muffins, soups, meat dishes, and of course salads. Hats off to Mann Packing and all they do to make a healthier world!

Mann Packing Company is a leading grower of innovative, ready to eat fresh vegetables. The company is one of the world's largest suppliers of fresh broccoli. Mann grows, processes, and distributes more than thirty-five fresh vegetable items under the Sunny Shores brand, including Broccoli Wokly, Broccoli Cole Slaw, Vegetable Medley, Broccolini, California Stir Fry, Stringless Sugar Snap Peas, fresh cut Butternut Squash, and Sweet Potatoes. Mann also supplies the food service industry with over 20 field-packed commodities like cauliflower, romaine hearts, and Napa cabbage.

Cy Mann founded Mann Packing Company in 1939, and built it on a reputation of honesty and integrity. Family owned and operated for three generations, adherence to food safety, quality, and customer service can be found in every carton they grow, pack, and ship. Mann remains committed to increasing consumption of fresh vegetables on a daily basis. Seventy-seven percent of the shareholders are women who continue to promote the rich traditions and mission: Fresh Vegetables Made Easy.

www.veggiesmadeeasy.com

*Mann's Broccoli Cole Slaw is not just for salads!
This healthier version of seven-layer dip promises
to become a family favorite for dippers of all ages!*

Mann's Broccoli Cole Slaw Seven-Layer Dip

INGREDIENTS

1 31-ounce can or **2** 16-ounce cans fat-free refried beans

1 cup prepared salsa

1 12-ounce bag Mann's Broccoli Cole Slaw, chopped

2 cups cherry tomatoes, sliced

1 cup green onions, chopped

½ cup chopped cilantro

1 cup fat-free sour cream

Non-stick cooking spray

Fresh cut veggies or baked tortilla chips

Serves 10

INSTRUCTIONS

Spray the bottom of a 10- or 12-inch casserole dish with cooking spray.

Working in layers, begin by spreading refried beans evenly on the bottom of the casserole dish.

Next, spread an even layer of salsa over the beans.

Then spread a layer of a half-bag of raw, chopped broccoli cole slaw, sour cream, tomatoes, onions, and cilantro over the salsa.

End with a layer of broccoli cole slaw.

Cover the dish with plastic food wrap, and chill in the refrigerator for at least one hour.

Serve with a variety of fresh-cut veggies or baked tortilla chips.

Note: This dip can also be chilled overnight and served the next day.

Making homemade salsa or Pico de Gallo has never been easier or more nutritious! Mann's Broccoli Cole Slaw gives this beloved classic a new twist!

Mann's Fresh and Easy Pico de Gallo

INGREDIENTS

1   12-ounce bag Mann's Broccoli Cole Slaw

1½ cups cilantro

1   7-ounce can chopped green chilies, undrained

3   cloves garlic

3   fresh Roma tomatoes, unpeeled

2   Tbsp. lime juice

1   14.5-ounce can low-sodium stewed tomatoes, undrained

½   tsp. salt

Optional: ½ seeded jalapeño pepper

Serves 5 or more

INSTRUCTIONS

Combine all ingredients in a food processor. Pulse until mixture reaches desired salsa consistency. Serve with sugar snap peas instead of high-calorie chips!

Store leftover salsa in the refrigerator.

> *Mix ½-cup of this Pico de Gallo with ¼ cup of low-fat ranch dressing for a super low-calorie salad dressing that thoroughly satisfies the craving for a creamy, rich dressing!*

This healthy snack is a great substitute for taco or barbecue-flavored chips!

Taco-Flavored Snappys

INGREDIENTS

1 8-ounce bag Mann's Sugar Snap Peas

1 Tbsp. taco- or mesquite-flavored dried seasoning

Cooking spray, plain or butter-flavored

Makes 2-½ servings

INSTRUCTIONS

Open the bag of sugar snap peas and spray a light coating of cooking spray over peas. Immediately add the dried seasoning to the bag. Hold the bag tightly shut and shake until the sugar snap peas are well coated.

Serve with hot dogs, hamburgers, or sandwiches.

For cheese-flavored Snappys, sprinkle grated Parmesan cheese over peas instead of taco seasoning.

Calorie Saver: Taco-Flavored Snappys are only 40 calories per serving. Three ounces of barbecue potato chips are about 400 calories!

Chopped Broccoli Cole Slaw adds fiber, crunch, and color to this delicious tuna sandwich! Using the liquid from the dill pickles instead of high-fat mayo cuts the calorie content dramatically and adds tons of flavor!

Broccoli Cole Slaw Tuna Salad

INGREDIENTS

1 12-ounce can of chunk light tuna in water (drained)

1 cup Mann's Broccoli Cole Slaw (chopped, raw)

1 Tbsp. light mayonnaise

1 Tbsp. prepared yellow mustard

1 large dill pickle (chopped)

2 Tbsp. pickle juice reserved from jar

10 slices whole-wheat bread

Salt and pepper to taste

Makes 5 sandwiches

INSTRUCTIONS

In a medium bowl, combine all ingredients (except bread).

Spoon tuna mixture evenly between five bread slices.

Add a second slice of bread to sandwiches, and cut in half to serve.

Mayo has 90 calories per tablespoon; yellow mustard has 0 calories; dill pickle juice has 0 calories.

Mann's Sweet Potato Cubes and Broccoli Cole Slaw, apples, cranberries, and cinnamon make this salad a perfect holiday recipe. And it's an ideal, make-ahead dish because it tastes better when served the next day!

Harvest Slaw Salad

INGREDIENTS

2 16-ounce bags Mann's Broccoli Cole Slaw

2 16-ounce bags Mann's Sweet Potato Cubes

1 cup dried cranberries

3 cups diced apples (skin on)

½ tsp. garlic salt

½ tsp. ground cinnamon

1 cup fat-free ranch dressing or Dijon dressing

Serves 8 to 10

INSTRUCTIONS

Pierce the bag of sweet potato cubes with a knife and place in the microwave. Microwave on high for 3-½ minutes or until sweet potato cubes are tender. Allow to cool.

Place all ingredients in a large bowl and toss. Serve salad on a chilled plate or in a large lettuce leaf or cabbage shell.

This salad keeps well after it is dressed for three days in the refrigerator.

Wondering what to do with your holiday leftovers? Add leftover turkey to this salad and serve it as a post-holiday main course.

When you make this moist and juicy meatloaf for the family, the kids will have no idea that carrots, broccoli stalks, and cabbage are what make it taste so good!

"This recipe also works great for making hamburger patties!"

Edgar Escobar
Rancho Cielo Student

Broccoli Cole Slaw Meatloaf

INGREDIENTS

1 16-ounce bag Mann's Broccoli Cole Slaw

1 lb. ground turkey

1 lb. lean ground beef

½ yellow onion (finely chopped)

½ cup prepared BBQ sauce

1 envelope dried onion soup mix

2 eggs

Serves 6 to 8

INSTRUCTIONS

Heat oven to 350°.

Pierce the bag of broccoli cole slaw with a knife and place in the microwave. Microwave for 5 minutes or until tender. Allow slaw to cool before chopping and adding to other ingredients.

In a large bowl, combine all ingredients and mix well.

Place meat mixture in a 3-pound loaf pan, or shape meat mixture into a loaf and place in a 13" by 9" baking dish.

Bake uncovered at 350° for 50 to 60 minutes.
Note: Baking times may vary.

Using cooked Mann's Broccoli Cole Slaw instead of starchy pasta is one of my best-kept secrets!

I Can't Believe It's Not Pasta and Sauce!

INGREDIENTS FOR SAUCE

- **1** lb. lean ground beef
- **1** lb. turkey Italian sausage (bulk or out of casings)
- **1** 12-ounce bag Mann's Broccoli Cole Slaw
- **2** carrots, grated
- **5** garlic cloves, minced
- **1** large purple onion, chopped
- **2** 8-ounce baskets of sliced mushrooms

Serves 8

- **2** cups red wine
- **2** cups port wine
- **1** Tbsp. sea salt
- **1** Tbsp. rosemary, chopped
- **1** Tbsp. fresh sage leaves, chopped
- **1** Tbsp. ground allspice
- **3** Tbsp. olive oil
- **8** cups good quality jarred pasta sauce

INGREDIENTS FOR "I CAN'T BELIEVE IT'S NOT PASTA"

- **2** 12-ounce bags Mann's Broccoli Cole Slaw
- **½** cup grated Parmesan cheese

INSTRUCTIONS

Microwave one bag of broccoli cole slaw for 5 minutes. Allow to cool and then chop. Set cooled slaw aside.

In a large Dutch oven or soup pot, heat olive oil over medium-high heat.

Immediately add carrots, onions, and garlic to the olive oil, and cook until vegetables are tender. Add meats, mushrooms, and chopped broccoli cole slaw.

After the meats are browned, add the wines. Simmer the mixture until the wine evaporates and the meats are almost dry. Add sea salt, herbs, and allspice.

When meats have started sticking to the pan, add pasta sauce and stir until sauce is hot and flavors blend.

Microwave the two remaining bags of broccoli cole slaw for five minutes each. Pour the vegetables into a pasta bowl. Spoon the sauce over the cooked broccoli cole slaw. Sprinkle with grated Parmesan cheese.

> *This recipe makes a large pot of sauce, so you can freeze what's left and use it for another quick and nutritious weekday meal!*

Add Mann's Sweet Potatoes instead of meat to your chili and increase your vitamin A intake to 90 percent of your daily requirement!

Easy Sweet Potato Chili

INGREDIENTS

5 cups Mann's Sweet Potato Cubes or Sweet Potato Spears

2 15-ounce cans chili beans in chili gravy

1 30-ounce can whole black beans, drained

½ cup prepared BBQ sauce

¼ tsp. ground allspice

Optional toppings: low-fat grated cheddar cheese, low-fat sour cream, chopped onions

Makes 8 servings

INSTRUCTIONS

Place the bag of sweet potato cubes or spears in the microwave and cook for 5 minutes or until sweet potatoes are tender.

In a large soup pot, combine chili beans, black beans, BBQ sauce, and allspice. Cook over medium-high heat until hot and bubbling. Add cooked sweet potato cubes or chopped sweet potato spears to the beans. Continue cooking until bubbly again.

Serve in bowls with desired toppings.

Try adding cooked sweet potatoes to refried beans for added nutrition!

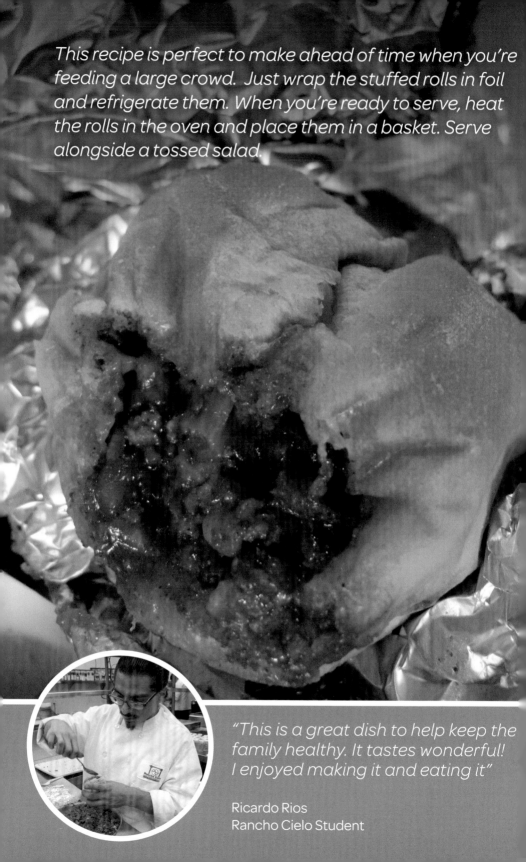

This recipe is perfect to make ahead of time when you're feeding a large crowd. Just wrap the stuffed rolls in foil and refrigerate them. When you're ready to serve, heat the rolls in the oven and place them in a basket. Serve alongside a tossed salad.

"This is a great dish to help keep the family healthy. It tastes wonderful! I enjoyed making it and eating it"

Ricardo Rios
Rancho Cielo Student

Mann's Dinner in a Bun

INGREDIENTS

1 1-lb. bag Mann's Broccoli Cole Slaw, cooked and chopped

1 lb. lean ground beef or ground turkey

1 tsp. garlic salt

1 cup sliced black olives (drained)

½ cup prepared BBQ sauce

½ tsp. ground allspice

10 small french or sourdough rolls

1 cup low-fat grated cheddar cheese (optional)

Makes 10 stuffed rolls

INSTRUCTIONS

Preheat oven to 350°.

Cut 10 squares of aluminum foil

Pierce the bag of broccoli cole slaw with a knife and place in the microwave. Microwave on high for 5 minutes or until broccoli cole slaw is tender.

In a large sauté pan, over medium-high heat, crumble and brown meat. Season with garlic salt. After meat is cooked (no longer pink), turn off the heat and mix in the cooked broccoli cole slaw, olives, cheese, BBQ sauce, and allspice. Set aside slaw meat mixture.

Make a small hole on one side of each roll and pull out the soft middle of bread, leaving the roll hollow. Fill each roll with 3 to 4 teaspoons of slaw meat mixture. Wrap each stuffed roll in a square of foil, and then place the rolls in a 350° oven for 10 to 15 minutes.

Serve rolls wrapped in foil and placed in a basket.

MAKE AND BAKE LATER

After stuffing the rolls, wrap them in foil and store them in the refrigerator until you're ready to heat them in the oven. Increase heating time to 20 minutes, or heat until the centers of the rolls are piping hot.

Use Mann's Butternut Squash in place of oil in these tasty, easy-to-make muffins. The squash reduces the calorie count and increases the nutritional value. Just watch how quickly these muffins disappear!

Easy Butternut and Spice Muffins

INGREDIENTS

1 18-ounce carrot or spice packaged cake mix

1 cup water

4 egg whites or 3 whole eggs

1 cup Mann's Butternut Squash Cubes

Optional: chopped nuts, coconut, raisins, butterscotch chips

Makes 24 muffins

INSTRUCTIONS

Preheat oven to 350°.

Cook butternut squash cubes according to directions on package. Set aside to cool.

In a large mixing bowl, combine the cake mix, water, egg whites (or eggs), and cooked squash. Mix at medium speed for two minutes, scraping bowl often. Add the optional ingredients as desired and fold into batter. Place cupcake papers in a muffin tin and fill each $2/3$ full with batter.

Bake muffins at 350° for 20 minutes. Serve warm or at room temperature.

Make these muffins even tastier by dusting them with powdered sugar, or by topping each one with a dollop of non-dairy whipped cream.

> *One-half cup of vegetable oil used in a cake mix can be over 900 calories, while one cup of cooked butternut squash is only 82 calories with no fat!*

For a quick and satisfying breakfast, use Mann's pre-cut sweet potatoes for a healthy choice. This scrambler is low in fat and my favorite substitute for starchy white potatoes.

Egg and Sweet Potato Scrambler

INGREDIENTS

1 16-ounce bag Mann's Sweet Potato Cubes

4 veggie sausage patties, cooked and chopped

8 eggs, lightly beaten (or use egg substitute)

Salt and pepper to taste

Fat-free sour cream, fresh salsa, and chopped green onions (for garnish)

Salt and pepper to taste

Non-stick cooking spray

Serves 4 to 6

INSTRUCTIONS

Pierce the bag of sweet potato cubes with a knife and place in the microwave. Microwave on high for 3-½ minutes or until sweet potato cubes are tender.

Spray a large skillet with cooking spray. Over medium-high heat, sauté sweet potato cubes, sausage, and eggs. Cook until eggs are well set. Add salt and pepper to taste.

Serve with a dollop of sour cream, salsa, and a sprinkle of onions.

This is the crowning glory of all my recipes! It is hands-down the most requested recipe at my Chef demonstrations. My Rancho Cielo students were excited when they found out how easy these meatballs are to make! They served them on a bed of fresh baby spinach instead of starchy pasta, and our guests loved it!

"These meatballs tasted so good, I surprised myself when I finished making them."

Reyna Gabot
Rancho Cielo Student

Broccoli Cole Slaw Meatballs

INGREDIENTS

1 16-ounce bag Mann's Broccoli Cole Slaw

1 lb. ground turkey or lean ground beef
(1 ½ lb. of meat works well in this recipe also)

½ cup parsley, finely chopped

5 tsp. grated Parmesan cheese

2 tsp. garlic salt

2 tsp. dried Italian seasoning

2 tsp. garlic and herb flavored salt-free seasoning

1 egg

Cooking spray

Makes approximately 15 average-sized meatballs and 30 mini meatballs

INSTRUCTIONS

Preheat oven to 350°.

Pierce the bag of broccoli cole slaw with a knife and place in the microwave. Microwave for 5 minutes or until tender. Allow to cool and then chop.

In a large bowl, combine all ingredients and mix.

Prepare a baking sheet with cooking spray. Shape meat mixture into 1½" balls (I use a small ice-cream scoop) and place them on the baking sheet.

Bake the meatballs in a hot oven for 30 minutes and serve. If making mini meatballs, reduce the baking time to 15-to-18 minutes.

> *Using cooked Mann's Broccoli Cole Slaw instead of breadcrumbs adds nutrients and creates a tender moist meatball that the entire family will love!*

SAGE FRUIT COMPANY

My dream come true is to teach healthy family cooking at our log lodge in the state of Washington, and I naturally gravitate to the beautiful fruits of the Yakima region.

The Sage Fruit Company has provided me with some of the most luscious fruits to inspire new recipes and to use in my educational cooking demonstrations at schools. Kids of all ages have helped me come up with many recipes using apples, pears, cherries and peaches, and as we all know, if children play a part in the preparation of home-cooked meals, they are surely going to enjoy eating the results!

Sage Fruit Company is made up of three family businesses from Central Washington. They are Valley Fruit in Wapato, Olympic Fruit in Moxee, and Larson Fruit in Selah. Together, the owners of these companies farm several thousands of acres of orchard ground and serve additional high-quality growers who entrust their fruit to Sage. While Sage is made up of families who came to Yakima long ago to farm, Sage Fruit Company itself began operations in 1999, when these family grower-shippers found it would be beneficial to join forces in order to provide consistent year-round supplies to their customers. Today, Sage Fruit Company ships fruit across the globe to Asia, Europe, South America, Mexico, and Canada in addition to retailers across the U.S. They deliver some of the world's most healthy foods from one of the world's most fertile growing regions. Today, Sage Fruit Company is considered one of the premier grower-shippers in the world for apples, pears, and cherries.

www.sagefruit.com

This is a wonderful after-school treat for children. They get fiber from the apples and calcium from the dip!

Crunchy Apple and Butterscotch Dippers

INGREDIENTS

4 Sage Sonya Apples

1 lemon, juiced

1¼ cups nonfat or low-fat milk

1 3.4-oz box instant butterscotch pudding

1 envelope dry whipped topping mix

Makes 4 one-half cup servings

INSTRUCTIONS

Rinse and dry the apples. Slice with skin on.

Place apple slices in a medium-sized bowl. Squeeze the lemon juice over apples and toss to coat. Set aside.

In a medium-sized electric mixer bowl, add milk, pudding mix, and dry whipped topping. Mix on high for two minutes or until dip is thick, creamy, and well-combined.

Spoon dip into small custard cups and serve with apple slices for dipping.

Store leftover dip in the refrigerator.

For variety of dips, try other flavors of instant pudding!

For a perfect holiday dish, add fresh pears to your favorite salad!

Sage Fresh Pear and Baby Greens Salad

INGREDIENTS

Salad

1 15-ounce bag baby greens

1 red Sage D'Anjou Pear

1 tsp. lemon juice

1 cup seedless red grapes (rinsed, dried, and cut in half)

1 ounce crumbled blue cheese

3 ounces walnut pieces

3 ounces dried cranberries

Salad Dressing

½ cup apple cider vinegar

2 Tbsp. extra virgin olive oil

1 Tbsp. Dijon mustard

2 Tbsp. maple syrup

Serves 6

INSTRUCTIONS

Rinse and dry the pear. Leaving skin on, cut pear into cubes.

Place cubes in a small bowl and add lemon juice. Toss to coat. Set aside.

Prepare the salad dressing by combining apple cider vinegar, olive oil, Dijon mustard, and maple syrup in a large bowl. Whisk ingredients together until well combined.

Combine baby greens, pears, and grapes in a large salad bowl or on a serving platter. Garnish with blue cheese, walnuts, and cranberries.

Dress and toss the salad just before serving.

This guilt-free apple turnover is much healthier than store-bought toaster pastries.

Skinny Breakfast Apple Turnovers

INGREDIENTS

Whole-wheat pita bread, 2 pieces cut in half (4 pockets)

2   Sage cooking Apples: Sonya, Fuji, or Honey Crisp (skin on)

1   Tbsp. maple syrup

¼   tsp. ground cinnamon

4   Tbsp. low-fat whipped cream cheese

Makes 4 turnovers

INSTRUCTIONS

Apples

Rinse, core, and slice apples.

Sprinkle apple slices with cinnamon and place in a microwavable dish. Add maple syrup.

Cover the dish with a lid or microwavable food wrap and microwave on high for two minutes.

Stir and microwave for an additional minute or until apples are tender.

Pita pockets

Toast pita halves.

Spread 1 tablespoon of cream cheese inside each pita pocket.

Divide apples into four equal portions and scoop into pita pockets.

Serve and enjoy!

> *For an even lower-calorie version, omit the cream cheese.*

Sliced Gala apples add flavor and crunch to any sandwich. I use apples in my sandwiches instead of cheese!

Turkey and Fresh Apple Sandwiches

INGREDIENTS

1 Sage Gala Apple

4 slices deli-style turkey breast

4 lettuce leaves

4 slices whole-wheat bread

1 Tbsp. light mayonnaise

2 Tbsp. prepared mustard

Makes 4 half sandwiches

INSTRUCTIONS

Rinse, core, and slice apple very thin.

Combine mayonnaise and mustard in a small bowl and spread mixture on bread slices.

Place apples, turkey, and lettuce on one slice of bread, and top with a second slice.

Cut sandwich in half and enjoy!

Did you know that one tablespoon of regular mayonnaise has 100 calories, and yellow mustard has zero calorie?

This is a standout appetizer that will make any holiday event more memorable. I recommend you use the Comice pear, which is one of the juiciest and most flavorful pears available. The Comice originated in France and adds sophistication to these festive appetizer wraps.

Sophisticated Pear and Salmon Lettuce Wraps

INGREDIENTS

1 Sage Comice Pear, skin on

12 butter lettuce leaves, rinsed and dried

4 ounces smoked salmon, cut into 12 equal pieces

1 cup low-fat, herb-flavored spreadable cheese

Makes 12 wraps

INSTRUCTIONS

Rinse and dry the pear. Cut into 12 slices. Set aside.

Rinse and dry the lettuce leaves and place them side by side.

To assemble wraps

Spread one spoonful of soft cheese down the center of each lettuce leaf.

Place one pear slice on top of each spoonful of cheese.

Top each pear slice with a piece of smoked salmon.

Fold each lettuce leaf taco style to create a wrap, and place each wrap close together on a serving plate.

For convenience, you can make these wraps two hours ahead of time, cover with plastic food wrap, and store in the refrigerator until you are ready to serve.

Fresh apples are filled with fiber, and yogurt is a good source of protein.

Fresh Apple Breakfast Parfait

INGREDIENTS

2   Sage Sonya Apples

½   lemon, juiced

2   6-ounce containers low-fat vanilla yogurt, or plain Greek yogurt

½   cup protein and fiber cereal (honey, almond, and flax multigrain cereal)

Makes 2 parfaits

INSTRUCTIONS

Rinse and dry the apples. Dice with the skin on.

Place diced apples in a medium-sized bowl. Add lemon juice and toss to coat.

In each parfait glass, add a layer of diced apples followed by one container of yogurt and another layer of apples. Top with cereal.

Serve and enjoy!

For a healthy and quick breakfast, prepare these parfaits the night before. Cover them with plastic food wrap and store them in the refrigerator.

Make these quick and easy low-fat muffins for a tasty breakfast on the run!

Pear Oatmeal Raisin Muffins

INGREDIENTS

1   packaged yellow cake mix

1⅓ cups water

1   fresh, very ripe Pear (peeled, cored, and chopped)

2   large eggs

2   cups quick oats

1   cup raisins

½   cup chopped nuts (walnuts or pecans)

1½ tsp. ground cinnamon

Makes 24 muffins

INSTRUCTIONS

Preheat oven to 350°.

Line a muffin pan with 24 paper muffin cups.

In a large bowl, mix together cake mix, water, chopped pear, eggs, and oats until well blended. Stir in raisins, nuts, and cinnamon.

Fill each muffin cup ¾ full of batter.

Bake 20 to 25 minutes and serve warm from the oven.

Use one fresh ripe pear instead of oil or fat in any muffin recipe for a healthier muffin!

Healthy apples and oatmeal come together to make this slow-cooker breakfast a family favorite!

Slow-Cooker Apple Oatmeal Custard Breakfast

INGREDIENTS

4 cups water or sugar-free apple juice (heated to boiling)

3 cups uncooked quick-cooking oats

3 cups peeled Sage Apples (chopped and cored)

½ tsp. salt

1 tsp. ground cinnamon

Serves 8

6 egg yolks

½ cup granulated sugar

2 cups low-fat evaporated milk

1 tsp. vanilla

¼ cup packed brown sugar

Nonstick cooking spray

INSTRUCTIONS

Coat slow-cooker with cooking spray. Cover and set on high to heat.

Pour hot apple juice into preheated slow-cooker.

Stir in oats, salt, apples, and cinnamon. Cover slow-cooker.

Over stove, heat milk and vanilla on medium heat until mixture begins to simmer. Remove from heat.

Combine eggs and granulated sugar in a bowl.

Whisk ½ cup of the hot milk into egg mixture. Whisk warm egg mixture into the remaining milk.

Pour mixture over the oatmeal and apples. Do not stir.

Turn slow-cooker to low and line the lid with 2 paper towels. Cover and cook on low for 3 to 3½ hours.

Uncover and sprinkle with brown sugar and serve.

Oatmeal and apples are excellent sources of fiber!

This light-as-air pancake makes a perfect holiday breakfast.

Pear Ricotta Pancakes

INGREDIENTS

Dry

1 cup all-purpose flour

1¼ tsp. baking powder

½ tsp. ground nutmeg

Wet

2 ripe Sage Bosc Pears

1¼ cup low-fat ricotta cheese

4 tsp. sugar

2 eggs

¾ cup nonfat milk

Juice from one lemon

Toppings

Sugar-free pancake syrup

2 cups chopped pecans

Makes 15 pancakes

INSTRUCTIONS

Peel, core, and dice the pears.

Place pears in a microwaveable container and cover with a lid or microwavable food wrap. Microwave for two minutes or until tender. Remove the lid and allow pears to cool.

In a medium bowl, combine the dry ingredients and set aside.

In a large bowl, use an electric mixer to combine wet ingredients (except pears).

With a mixing spoon, fold in the dry ingredients and half of the cooked pears into the ricotta mixture. Do not overmix. Use the remaining pears to garnish the pancakes.

Heat a nonstick skillet or griddle to 350° (medium heat). Spray skillet with cooking spray.

Use a ladle to pour ¼ cup of batter onto the hot skillet. Cook one side of the pancakes until bubbles form on top, and then flip and continue cooking until pancakes are golden brown.

Plate pancakes and top each stack with a spoonful of cooked pears and chopped pecans. Serve with warm pancake syrup.

Grilled peaches with frozen yogurt is a healthier option than pie with ice cream—and every bit as delicious!

Sage Grilled Peaches with Vanilla Frozen Yogurt

INGREDIENTS

Vanilla Frozen Yogurt

4 cups non-fat vanilla yogurt

½ cup sugar

1 tsp. vanilla extract

Grilled Peaches

6 ripe Sage Peaches

½ cup honey

Serves 12

INSTRUCTIONS

Frozen yogurt

For this recipe, you will need to use an ice-cream maker, either electric or manual, and follow the manufacturer's directions to make ice cream.

In a large bowl, combine yogurt, sugar, and vanilla extract. Pour mixture into the ice-cream machine. If using a hand crank , add ice and rock salt to the bucket and turn handle until it becomes difficult to turn (about 20 to 30 minutes).

Scoop frozen yogurt into a freezer-safe container with a lid, and place in the freezer.

Grilled peaches

To prepare peaches for grilling, rinse and pat dry, slice in half, and remove pits.

Place prepared peaches, sliced side up, on a baking tray and brush with honey.

Heat an outdoor or indoor grill.

Place peach halves, sliced side down, on the hot grill. Grill for one minute or until grill lines form. Turn over and grill the other side until skins begins to pull away from the peaches.

Remove peaches from the grill and serve peach halves with frozen yogurt.

Photo by Ocean Mist Farm

OCEAN MIST FARMS®

I live minutes from some of the most stunning fields of artichokes in the world. Every time I pass these majestic plants, I say a prayer for all of the people that dedicate their lives to growing, harvesting, and delivering this beautiful vegetable to our tables. It is very hard work, and I am grateful for farms that demonstrate pure heartfelt passion. For many years, I have had the privilege to experience Ocean Mist Farms® and that passion. I am honored to provide them with my services in order to educate consumers. I would have to say that talking about artichokes is one of my most favorite things to do in my career and what an honor it is to travel around the United States and Canada and introduce families to the artichoke. I can talk about the artichoke for hours...and I have!

Photo by Ocean Mist Farm

Since 1924, Ocean Mist Farms® has provided Americans with the freshest artichokes and vegetables, and continues to be family owned and operated today. Located in Castroville, California, the "artichoke capitol of the world" and home of the annual Castroville Artichoke Festival, Ocean Mist Farms® is the largest grower of fresh artichokes in North America.

One of the oldest-known foods, artichokes have delighted and nourished people for several thousands of years. Today, artichokes are enjoyed in every corner of the globe, and Ocean Mist Farms® is proud to produce the best quality and tastiest varieties available anywhere.

In addition to artichokes, Ocean Mist Farms® grows a full line of over 30 fresh vegetable commodities year-round in multiple growing regions with the most fertile ground and productive microclimates throughout California, Arizona, and Mexico. For more information and a library of recipes and cooking videos, visit www.oceanmist.com and join the artichoke club for a chance to win free field-fresh artichokes!

Ocean Mist and Ocean Mist Farms® is a registered trademark of California Artichoke and Vegetable Growers Corporation, A California corporation, and is used by permission.

Recipes and photographs are the property of California Artichoke and Vegetable Growers Corporation, a California corporation, and used by permission.

Ocean Mist Farms® creates guilt-free nachos that taste great! Artichoke leaves take the place of high-calorie tortilla chips. This is perfect as an appetizer or a satisfying main course.

Ocean Mist Farms® Artichoke Nachos

INGREDIENTS

2 whole Artichokes, cooked
(learn how to cook the perfect artichoke at www.oceanmist.com)

1½ cups low-fat refried beans, warmed

½ cup sliced cherry tomatoes

½ cup chopped green onions

½ cup salsa

½ cup chopped fresh cilantro

Serves 4 to 6

INSTRUCTIONS

Place cooked, cooled artichoke leaves in a single layer on a large platter. Save cooked artichoke hearts for another meal.

Spoon ½ teaspoon of warm beans onto each leaf. Top beans with tomatoes, onions, cilantro, and salsa. Add optional toppings as desired.

8 ounce of tortilla chips are about 900 calories, while 8 ounce of artichoke leaves are a low 40 calories!

Artichokes and garbanzo beans unite to make this flavorful dip!

Artichoke Hummus

INGREDIENTS

6 cooked Ocean Mist Farms® Artichokes (hearts, stems, and bottoms)
(learn how to cook the perfect artichoke at www.oceanmist.com)

½ cup light mayonnaise

Juice from one fresh lemon

2 Tbsp. olive oil

½ cup mild salsa

1 15 ounce can garbanzo beans (reserve liquid)

¼ cup grated Parmesan cheese

Salt and pepper to taste

Makes about 2½ cups of hummus

INSTRUCTIONS

In a food processor, combine all ingredients and pulse gradually, adding the liquid from the garbanzo beans, until the hummus is smooth.

Spoon hummus dip into cooked artichoke halves and enjoy with artichoke leaves or whole-wheat pita triangles. Refrigerate leftover hummus.

Visit www.oceanmist.com for more Ocean Mist Farms® vegetable recipes and cooking videos.

This incredible dish is a regular on my menu. I serve it alongside chicken, fish, or beef in place of rice and have no guilt piling a large helping on my plate!

I Can't Believe It's Not Rice

INGREDIENTS

1 head Ocean Mist Farms® Cauliflower

1 cup diced red bell pepper

3 chopped green onions

¼ cup chopped parsley

2 Tbsp. salt-free garlic and herb seasoning

Garlic salt to taste

Cooking spray

Serves 4 to 6

INSTRUCTIONS

Rinse the cauliflower under cold running water and pat dry. Cut into small pieces.

In a food processor, or using a sharp chef's knife, finely chop the cauliflower until it is slightly larger than grains of rice. Set aside.

Over medium-high heat, spray a large sauté pan with cooking spray. Add red bell pepper, parsley, and onions; cook until tender. Spray the pan with additional cooking spray, and then add chopped cauliflower. Add seasoning and sauté uncovered until cauliflower is tender (about 15 minutes). The more time you allow the cauliflower to cook, the fluffier it will become.

Note: Cooking the cauliflower uncovered will prevent it from becoming mushy.

> *Get creative with this recipe! Add chopped pineapple, Asian seasoning, and shrimp or chicken for Asian-style rice. You can also use this recipe as a base for Seafood paella—just add saffron, peas, sausage, and seafood!*

This award-winning concept is a real favorite with kids! Dipping artichoke leaves in chili is tasty and fun!

"This is a recipe that I will make for my family because it is healthy, delicious, and my family LOVES artichokes."

Joseph Reyna
Rancho Cielo Student

Ocean Mist Farms®
Chokes "n" Chili

INGREDIENTS

4 cups homemade chili or
2 16 ounce cans of your favorite chili beans

4 whole-cooked Artichokes
(visit www.oceanmist.com for cooking instructions)

1 cup low-fat grated cheddar cheese

Serves 4

INSTRUCTIONS

Over medium-high heat, warm chili beans in a medium-sized saucepan.

Divide chili between four bowls and top with ¼ cup of the grated cheese.

Serve the artichokes, using the leaves to dip into the chili. You can also fill the center of the cooked artichoke with chili for an attractive, edible chili bowl.

This is a fiber-rich meal that is so fun to eat! Cook artichokes ahead of time and store them in gallon sized food storage bags in the refrigerator. When ready to serve, fill artichokes with your favorite canned chili or better yet, use your own homemade chili.

This recipe will amaze you because it has the look and taste of real risotto!

Slow-Cooker Cauliflower Risotto

INGREDIENTS

2 heads Ocean Mist Farms® Cauliflower
(chopped raw to resemble grains of rice)

1½ cups vegetable or chicken broth

1 cup grated Parmesan cheese

Garlic salt and pepper to taste

1 cup frozen green peas (optional garnish)

Serves 4 to 6

INSTRUCTIONS

Set a slow-cooker on high. Fill with chopped cauliflower and broth. Add garlic salt, pepper, and one half of the Parmesan cheese. Stir with a large spoon to combine all ingredients.

Cover the crock-pot with a lid and cook for 3 to 3½ hours. After cooked to desired doneness, add frozen peas and toss. Serve cauliflower risotto with remaining grated Parmesan cheese and enjoy!

There are 204 calories in 1 cup of rice and only 25 calories in 1 cup of cauliflower!

Visit www.oceanmist.com for more Ocean Mist Farms® vegetable recipes and cooking videos.

You will never make stuffed potatoes without adding cauliflower again! These are delicious and full of nutrients.

"It's super awesome, delicious, and finger-licking good! And it's easy to make!

Delfina Valverde
Rancho Cielo Student

Cauliflower Stuffed Potatoes

INGREDIENTS

3 extra large baking potatoes (rinsed and dried)

1 head Ocean Mist Farms® Cauliflower (cut into quarters)

½ tsp. garlic salt

2 Tbsp. low-fat sour cream

½ cup vegetable or chicken broth, warmed

1 envelope dried onion soup mix

½ cup low-fat shredded cheddar cheese

Serves 6

INSTRUCTIONS

Preheat oven to 350°.

Place quartered cauliflower on a large sheet of heavy-duty foil. Season with garlic salt. Fold the foil into a packet, crimping the edges to seal. Place the packet in an ovenproof dish and place in a hot oven.

Pierce the skin of the potatoes and place them in the hot oven, next to the cauliflower packet.

Bake cauliflower and potatoes for 1 hour or until very tender when pierced with knife or fork. Remove the packet from the oven.

Remove the potatoes from the oven and cut them lengthwise. Scoop the hot contents into a large mixing bowl. Place the empty potato skins in an ovenproof casserole dish.

Add the baked cauliflower to the potatoes in the mixing bowl. Then add warm broth, sour cream, and soup mix. With an electric mixer, whip potato and cauliflower mixture until light and fluffy, adding more warm broth if needed.

Scoop the whipped potato and cauliflower mixture into the six potato skins and top each potato with cheddar cheese.

Bake in a hot oven for 15 minutes or until the cheese is melted.

Visit www.oceanmist.com for more Ocean Mist Farms® vegetable recipes and cooking videos.

This cauliflower side dish is a welcome substitute for high-calorie Spanish rice and proves that healthy foods can taste great!

Easy Spanish Cauliflower Rice

INGREDIENTS

1 head Ocean Mist Farms® Cauliflower

1 cup diced red bell pepper

3 green onions, chopped

1 1.25-ounce package taco seasoning

1 15-ounce can whole black beans (rinsed and drained), optional

Cooking spray

Serves 4

TIP: I like to double this recipe because the cauliflower rice disappears quickly!

INSTRUCTIONS

Rinse cauliflower under cold running water and pat dry. Cut cauliflower into small sections. In a food processor, or using a sharp chef's knife, finely chop cauliflower until it looks a little larger than grains of rice. Set aside.

Over medium-high heat, spray a large sauté pan with cooking spray.

Add bell pepper and onions to the pan. Cook until tender. Add chopped cauliflower and spray pan again with cooking spray. Add dry taco seasoning and sauté until cauliflower is tender (about 15 minutes). The longer the cauliflower cooks, the fluffier it will become. (To prevent cauliflower from becoming mushy, do not cover pan while it is cooking.)

Add black beans to cauliflower mixture and stir. Serve warm.

Serve this Spanish cauliflower rice inside tacos, burritos, or along side enchiladas and your family will never know they are eating cauliflower!

Artichokes are naturally low in calories, but dipping them in mayo or butter really raises their calorie count! Try Skinny-Baked Artichokes for a delicious, healthy choice!

I like to store baked, cooled artichokes in gallon-sized zipper-lock bags in the refrigerator until I'm ready to eat them. Heat by grilling or warming them in the microwave, or just eat them cold. Baked artichokes will keep in the refrigerator for about five days.

Skinny–Baked Artichokes

INGREDIENTS

4 large Artichokes

2 cups vegetable or chicken broth

½ cup white wine (optional)

4 Tbsp. olive oil

1 Tbsp. lemon juice

2 Tbsp. minced garlic

1 Tbsp. dried herb blend seasoning

Garlic salt to taste

Four squares heavy-duty foil or a baking dish with heavy duty foil cover

Serves 4

INSTRUCTIONS

Preheat oven to 425°.

Rinse artichokes under cold water and pat dry.

In a medium-sized bowl, combine broth, wine, lemon juice, garlic, olive oil, dried herbs, and garlic salt. Set aside.

Trim each artichoke by removing the stem and trimming ½ inch of its top. Reserve the stems, as they are tasty to eat when cooked. Bake the artichokes using aluminum foil or a baking dish as follows:

Aluminum foil squares:

Place each artichoke in the middle of one foil square (stem side down) and use your fingers to open up the petals of the artichoke. Evenly pour the broth mixture into each artichoke. Pull the four corners of the foil square up around the artichoke and firmly secure by crimping it at the top of the artichoke to form an airtight pouch.

Baking dish:

Place all of the artichokes into the dish (stem side down). Use your fingers to open up the petals of each artichoke and evenly fill with the broth mixture. Cover the baking dish with foil so that the steam does not escape.

Place artichokes in a hot oven and bake for 60-to-70 minutes or until artichokes are very tender (but don't peek or you will release needed steam for perfectly baked artichokes).

Serve hot or cold.

I love weekend breakfasts. Paired with eggs and a lean breakfast meat, these hash browns allow me to enjoy a big American breakfast that is healthy!

Ocean Mist Farms® Cauliflower Hash Browns

INGREDIENTS

1 head of raw Ocean Mist Farms® Cauliflower

½ cup red bell pepper, chopped

½ cup green bell pepper, chopped

½ cup yellow onion, chopped

Seasoning salt or herb seasoning

Cooking spray

Serves 4

INSTRUCTIONS

Rinse head of cauliflower under cold water and pat dry. Cut into small sections.

Chop cauliflower with a sharp knife so it resembles small chunks of potato.

Over medium-high heat, spray a large skillet with cooking spray and add bell pepper and onion. Sauté vegetables until tender, about 5 minutes.

Add cauliflower to the skillet and spray with additional cooking spray. Add seasoning to taste. Sauté cauliflower until tender, about 15 minutes. Cook uncovered to prevent cauliflower from becoming mushy.

Serve with your favorite style of eggs and lean breakfast meat.

Cook whole artichokes before you go camping, and then later, simply warm them over a campfire for deliciously smoky chokes!

Campfire Artichokes

INGREDIENTS

6 Ocean Mist Farms® Artichokes, cooked and cooled
   (learn how to cook the perfect artichoke at www.oceanmist.com)

¼ cup olive oil or cooking spray

Salt and pepper, to taste

Seasoning choices: herb and garlic; mesquite; BBQ

Serves 6

INSTRUCTIONS

Prepare and heat the grill.

Brush cooked artichokes with olive oil, or spray them with cooking spray. Season with salt and pepper or other seasoning (my favorite is mesquite seasoning).

Place whole artichokes (or artichoke halves) directly on the grill. Allow one side to char over heat. Using tongs, turn artichokes and char the other side.

Remove artichokes from grill and place on a serving platter. Serve as is, enjoying the natural grilled flavor, or serve with your favorite dipping sauce.

> *You can also make these smoky chokes on the grill at home.*

Visit www.oceanmist.com for more Ocean Mist Farms® vegetable recipes and cooking videos.

Cauliflower takes the place of rice in this healthy chicken soup.

I Can't Believe It's Not Rice & Chicken Soup

INGREDIENTS

1 head Ocean Mist Farms® Cauliflower (chopped raw to resemble grains of rice)

4 stalks celery (chopped)

1 small yellow onion (chopped)

¼ cup fresh parsley (chopped)

2 cups cooked boneless-skinless chicken breasts (diced)

1 tsp. salt-free herb seasoning

1 tsp. Herbs de Provence

1 tsp. garlic salt

4 cans (14 ounces) chicken broth

Serves 4 to 6

INSTRUCTIONS

Place a large soup pot over medium-high heat and spray with cooking spray. Add celery, onion, and parsley to the pot; cook vegetables until tender.

Add the cauliflower to the pot and continue to cook until it is tender (add more cooking spray if needed). Add seasonings, chicken, and broth to the vegetables. Continue cooking, stirring occasionally.

Serve soup piping hot and enjoy!

Visit www.oceanmist.com for more Ocean Mist Farms® vegetable recipes and cooking videos.

My mother would make chorizo and eggs almost every weekend when I was a child. This is a healthier version of the same dish. It can be served in tortillas or, for an even lower-calorie dish, Romaine lettuce leaves.

Cauliflower Mexican Sausage Scrambler

INGREDIENTS

1 head Ocean Mist Farms® Cauliflower, chopped raw to resemble small potato chunks

1 Tbsp. mesquite or dry taco seasoning

6 eggs (lightly beaten)

Salt and pepper to taste

1 vegetarian chorizo sausage link

Cooking spray

Serves 3

INSTRUCTIONS

Spray a large skillet with cooking spray. Over medium-high heat, sauté cauliflower chunks until tender. Cook uncovered to prevent cauliflower from becoming mushy.

Add seasoning to taste.

Add chorizo to skillet and combine with cauliflower. Add eggs. Stir and cook until eggs are set.

This filling makes great breakfast burritos, too!

ROYAL ROSE

When I think of Royal Rose, I immediately think of my culinary visits to Italy.

I've learned some of my most valuable home-cooking lessons in the medieval towns of Tuscany. Fresh simplicity seems to be the key to the best cooks in Italy. Bitter greens are picked fresh daily and lightly tossed with olive oil the color of green moss—it sounds simple, but the taste is a memory that I will never forget. Beautiful leafy colors are picked from the fields and used in soups, stews, pasta dishes, and appetizers. Every time I hold Radicchio in my hands, I think of all the wonderful recipes that families in Italy make with this gorgeous vegetable. My chapter on Royal Rose brings the beauty of Italy to you through vegetables!

Royal Rose Radicchio has been adding fresh color to the "salad bowl of the world" in Salinas, California, since 1993, when Italian farmers Lucio Gomiero and Carlo Boscolo teamed up with Salinas Valley growers to bring seasonal radicchio to America year-round. Royal Rose LLC currently follows the sun through multiple growing regions to supply the emergent market with field-fresh radicchio from California, Florida, Arizona, and Mexico.

Led by company president Dennis Donohue, Royal Rose's "Fresher-Bigger-Better" program reflects an ongoing commitment to educating consumers about this powerful vegetable's versatility and nutritional value. Royal Rose is also committed to education and popularizing radicchio in the American marketplace. McDonald's now includes radicchio in its premium salads in many markets, and chefs all over the country have come to look beyond the salad, holding this versatile vegetable in high esteem and using it raw, grilled, or sautéed and in a variety of specialized dishes.

www.radicchio.com

The students at Rancho Cielo Culinary Academy received rave reviews when they served this elegant dish at a charity event in Monterey, California.

Royal Rose Minted Apple Chicken Salad in Fresh Radicchio Cups

INGREDIENTS

3 cups cooked, chopped chicken (three boneless-skinless chicken breasts)

1 apple (cored and chopped)

2 green onions (chopped)

¼ cup chopped red bell pepper

⅔ cup low-fat mayonnaise

¼ cup fresh mint leaves (chopped)

Royal Rose Radicchio leaves to use as salad cups, **10** large
(or 20 small, 2 leaves per cup)

Salt and pepper to taste

Makes about 10 salad cups

INSTRUCTIONS

Rinse and separate the radicchio leaves. Carefully pat them dry with paper towels, making sure to maintain their circular cup-like shape.

In a large bowl, mix the remaining ingredients.

Spoon the minted chicken salad into the radicchio cups and enjoy!

This is a wonderful recipe to take to a party, because the radicchio leaves do not wilt!

In Italy and France, eggs are used to make a satisfying lunch or a late-night supper. I love this recipe because the egg acts as a wonderful, warm dressing that infuses flavor into the veggies.

Egg and Radicchio Salad

INGREDIENTS

2 cups baby salad greens

1 cup shredded Royal Rose Radicchio

6 cooked, cooled green beans or French beans (asparagus spears may also be used)

1 egg (poached or prepared sunnyside up)

1 tsp. extra virgin olive oil

Salt and pepper

Makes 1 salad entrée

INSTRUCTIONS

On a large salad plate, arrange baby greens, radicchio, and green beans. Place cooked egg in the middle of the salad and drizzle olive oil over the salad. Season with salt and pepper to taste.

This salad also tastes great with Royal Rose Growers' French, Frisee' a lovely "frilly" green.

I admire the home cooks in Italy because they don't throw anything away. This recipe helps American families put that wise and cost effective habit into practice.

Fit-for-a-Queen Turkey and Radicchio Soup

INGREDIENTS

1 cooked turkey breast carcass

6 cups chicken broth or enough water or broth to cover carcass in a soup pot

4 carrots, roughly chopped

6 celery stalks, roughly chopped

4 garlic cloves, minced

½ head green cabbage, shredded

1 head Royal Rose Radicchio, shredded (1 cup reserved for garnish)

Serves 12

1 tsp. garlic salt

1 tsp. salt-free herb seasoning

2 dried bay leaves

1 Tbsp. fresh oregano leaves, minced

2 Tbsp. fresh parsley, chopped

1 Tbsp. fresh rosemary, chopped

1 yellow onion, chopped

1 cup cooked brown rice (optional)

Salt and pepper to taste

INSTRUCTIONS

Place cooked turkey carcass in a large soup pot. Add enough broth to cover the carcass.

Add the remaining ingredients to the pot. Bring the soup to a boil, and then reduce heat and simmer for 2 hours.

Remove the turkey carcass and the bay leaves from the soup.

Spoon soup into bowls and garnish with shredded radicchio.

> *A turkey carcass and green cabbage is the base for this soup. Shredded radicchio makes a nickel-saving soup that is fit for a queen. Hats off to Royal Rose for growing such a regal vegetable!*

Royal Rose Radicchio No-Noodle Lasagna

INGREDIENTS

- **6** medium-sized zucchini, thinly sliced (a mandolin works well)
- **1** head Royal Rose Radicchio, shredded
- **1** large purple onion, chopped
- **1** red bell pepper, chopped
- **1** carrot, grated
- **3** cloves garlic, minced
- **1** 2-lb., 13-ounce jar Italian pasta sauce
- **1 lb.** ground turkey Italian sausage
- **2** cups low-fat ricotta cheese
- **1** egg

Makes 12 servings

- **1** 10-ounce box frozen chopped spinach (cooked, cooled, and drained)
- **½** cup Parmesan cheese for ricotta mixture
- **½** cup Parmesan cheese for top of lasagna
- **¼** cup fresh parsley, chopped
- **¼** tsp. nutmeg
- **3** cups shredded low-fat mozzarella cheese
- **2** Tbsp. olive oil
- **4** to **6** fresh basil leaves, chopped
- **1** Tbsp. fresh rosemary, chopped
- **1** tsp. garlic salt

Your family will never guess that this lasagna has no noodles in it at all! It tastes great and it's loaded with fresh-cooked veggies, so everyone can have second helpings of this flavorful dish without feeling guilty!

INSTRUCTIONS

Preheat oven to 350°.

In a large sauté pan over medium-high heat, add olive oil, onion, bell pepper, carrot, radicchio, basil, rosemary, garlic salt, and garlic. Cook until veggies are very tender. Add ground turkey to veggies and cook until turkey is no longer pink. Add pasta sauce to meat mixture and heat through. Set aside.

In a small bowl, mix ricotta cheese, Parmesan cheese, parsley, nutmeg, egg, and spinach until well combined. Set aside.

Using a mandolin or sharp knife, slice raw zucchini lengthwise to match the thickness of a raw lasagna noodle.

Spray the sides and bottom of a 9" x 13"-inch lasagna pan with cooking spray.

Begin layering the lasagna with a ladle of sauce in the bottom of the pan. Arrange sliced zucchini in a single layer over the sauce. Top zucchini with half of the ricotta cheese mixture, and sprinkle with one cup of the mozzarella. Next, ladle half of the sauce, followed by another layer of zucchini. Repeat ricotta cheese, mozzarella, and another layer of zucchini. Evenly spoon the remaining sauce over the last layer of zucchini, and sprinkle with mozzarella and Parmesan cheese.

Spray heavy-duty foil with cooking spray. Cover lasagna with foil and place casserole on a baking sheet. Bake in oven for one hour or until zucchini is very tender.

Uncover lasagna and continue to bake until the top is browned (about 15 to 20 minutes). Remove lasagna from oven and let cool. It should set in about 30 minutes.

Just like regular lasagna, this dish is more flavorful when made the day before you serve it.

Put everything in a slow cooker before work and come home to a delicious and healthy meal that tastes like a chef prepared it!

Slow-Cooker Radicchio Asian Wraps

INGREDIENTS

2 pounds raw boneless-skinless chicken breasts (finely chopped)
½ head Royal Rose Radicchio (shredded and finely chopped)
1 yellow onion (chopped)
6 cloves garlic (minced)
1 cup chopped water chestnuts
⅓ cup soy sauce
½ tsp. garlic salt
½ cup sweet cooking rice wine or apple juice
1 Tbsp. ground allspice
1 tsp. ground ginger
16 to **20** whole radicchio leaves

Garnish
1 carrot (grated)
3 green onions (chopped)
Prepared plum sauce or peanut sauce

Makes 16 to 20 wraps

INSTRUCTIONS

Place all of the ingredients (except radicchio leaves and plum sauce) in a 4- to 6-quart slow cooker. Mix well to combine the ingredients.

Cover the slow cooker with a lid and cook the mixture on a low setting for 6 hours, or on a high setting for 4 hours.

Spoon the warm mixture into the whole radicchio leaves. Add vegetable garnishes.

Serve warm with plum or peanut sauce.

> *This also makes a great appetizer! I love using radicchio for the wraps, because the leaves don't wilt when you add a hot filling to them.*

DRISCOLL'S BERRIES

Since I was a little girl, I've loved berries! I would choose fresh berries over chocolate any day! As long as I can remember, my birthday cake in July had to be filled with fresh strawberries. I even started developing recipes for fresh berries at a very young age, maybe eight or nine years old. I always tell my friends that when I enter heaven, I will be gifted with my very own berry patch!

As an adult, it is a real joy to know that one of my favorite childhood foods is really good for me. My weekly market trips always include a large quantity of fresh berries. They satisfy my sweet tooth cravings and offer me a variety of health benefits.

Driscoll's®

ONLY THE FINEST BERRIES™

For over 100 years, Driscoll's has been growing Only The Finest Berries™. In 1896 friends Joseph "Ed" Reiter, and R.O. Driscoll began producing Sweet Briar strawberries in California's Pajaro Valley. Four generations later, the tradition of family farming continues today as Driscoll's partners with independent growers around the world to provide a complete berry patch of conventional and organic strawberries, blueberries, raspberries and blackberries to the delight of berry lovers everywhere. Driscoll's berries are known for the their superior flavor, appearance, and quality and each one is packed with nutrition and antioxidants. Please enjoy Driscoll's berries as a part of your healthy lifestyle.

www.driscolls.com

Do you want a healthy start to your day? Try this breakfast salad alongside your favorite eggs! It's easy to prepare and it looks so pretty.

Driscoll's Healthy Berry Breakfast Salad

INGREDIENTS

1 large head butter lettuce or your favorite greens

1 basket fresh Driscoll's Raspberries or Strawberries

¼ cup cooked, crumbled turkey bacon

Salt and pepper to taste

1 avocado, sliced or cubed (optional)

Breakfast Salad Dressing

3 Tbsp. extra virgin olive oil

¼ cup fresh orange juice

½ tsp. fresh mint leaves, chopped (optional)

Serves 4 to 6

INSTRUCTIONS

Rinse berries under cold running water and pat dry. If using strawberries, also hull and slice.

Over a medium-sized bowl, tear butter lettuce into bite-size pieces. Add berries, crumbled bacon, avocado (optional), and salt and pepper. In a small bowl, combine olive oil, orange juice, and mint (optional) and whisk.

Drizzle dressing over the salad and toss gently.

Serve alongside your favorite omelet, scramblers, or frittatas.

This is my favorite dish to make for company. All of the flavors work so well together to make a beautiful and aromatic main course that is heart healthy!

Blueberry & Balsamic Herbed Chicken Breasts

INGREDIENTS

Balsamic Blueberry Reduction

2 cups good quality balsamic vinegar

2 cups fresh Driscoll's Blueberries (reserve ½ cup for garnish)

Herb Sautéed Chicken Breasts

4 boneless-skinless chicken breasts (pounded thin)

4 Tbsp. olive oil

4 cups baby spinach, rinsed and dried

1 tsp. garlic salt

1 Tbsp. Herbes de Provence

Serves 4

INSTRUCTIONS

In a small saucepan, bring vinegar to a boil and reduce heat to a simmer. Let the vinegar reduce to about 1 cup or a little less. Remove the pan from the heat and add 1 ½ cups blueberries. Set aside.

Season the chicken breasts with garlic salt and dried herbs.

Heat olive oil in a large skillet. Place the seasoned chicken in the hot oil and brown on both sides (about 3 minutes per side). Remove the chicken and place on a warm plate. Add blueberry reduction to the hot pan (heat should be off or very low). Use a spatula to loosen the tiny bits of chicken from the bottom of the sauté pan, and mix the bits into the sauce.

Put one quarter of the fresh spinach on each plate and top with a cooked chicken breast. Spoon the blueberry sauce over the chicken and garnish it with fresh blueberries. Serve immediately.

A great sauce doesn't have to include butter or cream!

Use angel food cupcakes for the short cakes, and substitute cran-raspberry juice for sugar in these tasty little berry gems!

Berry Light Short Cakes

INGREDIENTS

1 angel food packaged cake mix

3 cups sliced fresh Driscoll's Strawberries

3 cups fresh Driscoll's Blueberries

3 cups fresh Driscoll's Raspberries

4 cups non-dairy whipped topping (found in the freezer aisle)

3 cups sugar-free cran-raspberry juice

Makes 24 short cakes

INSTRUCTIONS

Prepare cake batter according to package directions.

Place paper baking cups in a muffin tin and spoon batter into baking cups.

Bake for about 20 minutes until cupcakes appear dry.

Let cool.

In a large bowl, combine berries and cran-raspberry juice.

Remove paper from cooled cupcakes.

Slice cupcakes in half horizontally. Place the bottom halves on a plate and spoon berry mixture onto each half. Top with the other half of the cupcake. Finish with a generous dollop of whipped topping, and garnish with more berries. Serve immediately.

There is only 52 calories in one plain angel food cupcake!

Create fresh strawberry frozen yogurt in minutes! Serve after 30 minutes of churning, or store freshly churned yogurt in an airtight container in the freezer until ready to enjoy!

Driscoll's Easy Low-Fat Frozen Strawberry Yogurt

INGREDIENTS

4 cups non-fat vanilla yogurt

16 ounces fresh Driscoll's Strawberries
(or 16 ounces fresh Driscoll's Raspberries)

½ cup sugar

1 tsp. vanilla extract

Makes over one quart

INSTRUCTIONS

Rinse strawberries under cold running water and pat dry.

Hull and slice the berries and place them in a large bowl. Add sugar to the berries and mix. Let the berries sit for 20 minutes to allow the sugar to dissolve and soak into the berries. With a potato masher or fork, mash the strawberries. Mix in yogurt and vanilla.

Pre-freeze the drum of a tabletop ice-cream maker according to the manufacturer's directions.

Pour the yogurt mixture into the ice-cream maker. Allow to churn for 30 minutes or until yogurt is very thick. Scoop the strawberry yogurt into a covered freezer container and freeze until ready to serve.

Try making fresh berry smoothies with the leftover frozen yogurt.

A very popular bakery in Santa Cruz County makes a cookie that resembles these scones. I wanted to develop a recipe that would be lower in calories than traditional scones, but would still satisfy my sweet tooth! I love the use of fresh strawberries in these yummy treats!

Driscoll's Very Berry Strawberry Scones

INGREDIENTS

2⅓ cups reduced-fat biscuit mix

⅔ cup non-fat milk plus ¼ cup milk for glazing scones

2 Tbsp. sugar

5 Tbsp. non-fat Greek plain yogurt (vanilla-flavored also tastes great)

1 cup finely chopped fresh Driscoll's Strawberries

1 Tbsp. melted butter

2 Tbsp. decorator's sparkle sugar (sold at craft or food specialty stores)

Makes 12 scones

INSTRUCTIONS

Preheat oven to 400°.

In a large bowl, combine biscuit mix with ⅔ cup of milk, sugar, butter, and yogurt. Use your hands or a large spoon to combine the ingredients (dough will be lumpy.) Add chopped strawberries to the dough. I find that using my hands works best for mixing in the strawberries. This way, I make sure not to mash the strawberries in the process.

Spray a baking sheet with non-stick cooking spray. Drop dough onto the baking sheet in 12 small mounds (an icecream scoop works well). Use the remaining milk to brush the top of the scones, and then sprinkle decorator's sugar on top of each one.

Bake for 12 to 18 minutes until tops are lightly browned.

Serve warm and store at room temperature for one day. Any leftover scones can be refrigerated and then warmed in the oven before eating.

Perfect to serve for a spring breakfast or a summer tea party!

These tarts are easy, pretty, and lower in calories than typical bakery tarts.

Driscoll's Easy Berry & Cream Tarts

INGREDIENTS

12 fresh Driscoll's Strawberries, rinsed and dried and cut in half

1 6-ounce basket of Driscoll's Blueberries (rinsed and dried)

¼ cup seedless raspberry or strawberry jam

1 package (4 servings) instant vanilla or lemon pudding

1 cup cold low-fat or non-fat milk

1 envelope dry whipped topping mix

8 ladyfingers (cut in half)

8 cupcake or tart baking papers

1 cup frozen whipped topping (thawed)

Serves 8

INSTRUCTIONS

In a mixing bowl, add pudding mix, dry whipped topping mix, and milk. Using an electric mixer, blend at a low speed for 1 minute and then increase speed to medium-high and continue to whip until pudding mixture is well combined and very thick (about 3 minutes). Set aside.

Flatten a baking paper with your hand. Place two ladyfinger halves side by side on the paper.

Top the ladyfingers with one heaping tablespoon of pudding mixture.

Garnish each tart with three strawberry halves and about nine blueberries.

In a small microwavable bowl, microwave the jam 5 to 8 seconds or until the jam is melted.

Use a small pastry brush to dab the jam glaze over the tops of the berries to give them a nice shine. Finish each tart with a dollop of whipped topping.

Store the tarts in the refrigerator for a few hours or overnight so that the ladyfingers soften.

> *To quicken the softening process of the ladyfingers and to add flavor, simply moisten the ladyfingers in a small amount of orange juice, sweet wine, or even cooled coffee!*

TAYLOR FARMS

You know how most people have bread as a staple in the kitchen for quick meals or snacks? Well, I have lettuce! The first thing that I teach in my cooking demos is that lettuce can take the place of high-calorie bread and it's as economical and accessible as any loaf of store-bought bread or bread products.

I love watching school-aged kids enjoy lettuce tacos and ask for more! And peanut butter and jelly on lettuce leaves is better than you might think! The great thing about lettuce is that you don't have to warm it or toast it—lettuce has a natural crunch that really satisfies.

I challenge you to look up the calorie content on your next slice of bread or flour tortilla and then look up the calorie content on a Romaine lettuce leaf; you will be pleasantly surprised to make the switch!

Taylor Farms provides us with an easy solution to a healthier America!

For over 80 years, Taylor Farms has been committed to healthy, wholesome produce. They are passionate about offering a collection of healthy, great tasting, fresh salads, vegetables, and snacks that are packed with nutrients and preservative-free. All of their produce is harvested at its peak of freshness and is thoroughly washed and ready to enjoy. Taylor Farms uses responsible, sustainable agriculture practices for everything they grow. Their salads and vegetables are grown by farmers that have the highest standards. By strategically aligning themselves with family farmers all over the nation, Taylor Farms has improved the freshness and quality of all your favorite products. Their number one priority is to provide fresh, wholesome produce that helps families live a healthier life.

www.taylorfarms.com

Romaine lettuce leaves are naturally shaped like a taco shell, so they hold carnitas and fajita fillings perfectly!

Taylor Farms Beef & Lettuce Fajitas

INGREDIENTS

2 pounds beef flank steak, cut into thin strips

1 package Taylor Farms Organic Romaine Heart Leaves (washed and ready to use)

1 medium yellow onion (thinly sliced)

1 medium green bell pepper (cut into thin strips)

1 medium red bell pepper (cut into thin strips)

1 package dry fajita seasoning

½ cup prepared mild salsa

Cooking spray

Makes 8 servings

INSTRUCTIONS

Heat a large skillet over medium-high heat. Lightly spray skillet with cooking spray. Place onions and peppers in hot skillet. Cook and stir vegetables about five minutes or until they are crisp-tender. Remove vegetables from skillet and set aside.

Place steak in hot skillet and add fajita seasoning; mix thoroughly. Cook steak for about 3 minutes or until cooked through. Add bell pepper mixture to steak and add salsa. Cook over heat and stir until fajita mixture is hot and well combined (about 2 minutes).

Fill lettuce leaves with fajitas and top with your favorite condiments. Serve immediately.

The easiest way to save calories is to substitute high-carb tortillas or taco shells with lettuce. Each corn or flour tortilla can have up to 150 calories each; one romaine lettuce leaf is less then 5 calories! I keep plenty washed and ready to eat in the family refrigerator.

The first healthy-eating lesson that I teach in schools is to use lettuce leaves instead of bread.

Taylor Farms Green Sandwiches

INGREDIENTS

8 Taylor Farms Green Leaf Singles (for Food Service use)

4 slices turkey breast

4 slices low-fat Swiss cheese

4 tomato slices

Prepared yellow mustard

Makes 4 sandwiches

INSTRUCTIONS

Place four of the lettuce leaves on a flat surface. Top each leaf with a slice of turkey, a slice of cheese, a tomato slice, and mustard. Get creative and add pickles, onions, or any other favorite veggies. Complete the sandwich with a second lettuce leaf and cut in half to serve.

When you use lettuce instead of bread, you save about 110 calories per slice of bread—that's over a 200 calorie savings per sandwich.

Whether you love traditional bean tostadas or this delicious recipe for chicken tostadas, using iceberg lettuce rounds cuts the prep time and the calories!

Easy Lettuce Tostadas

INGREDIENTS

1 large head Taylor Farms Iceberg Lettuce (rinsed and dried)

1 cooked rotisserie chicken (boned, skinned, and chopped)

1 15-ounce can fat-free refried beans (warmed)

1 red bell pepper (diced)

1 yellow onion (diced)

1 cup prepared mild salsa

½ cup prepared BBQ sauce

1 15-ounce can whole black or pinto beans, rinsed and drained (optional)

1 cup angel hair cabbage

1 cup chopped tomatoes

Cooking spray

Makes 6 servings

INSTRUCTIONS

Spray a large skillet with cooking spray and add onions and peppers. Cook vegetables over medium-high heat until peppers are tender. Add chicken, salsa, black beans, and BBQ sauce. Continue cooking until mixture is hot and well combined. Set aside.

Cut iceberg lettuce into 6 round circles and place on individual plates. Spread warmed refried beans on top of each lettuce round. Top beans with chicken mixture, and garnish with cabbage and tomatoes. Add salsa or taco sauce if desired. Serve immediately.

This is such an innovative and healthy way to serve tostadas, I'd love to see this dish offered in Mexican restaurants.

Instead of serving hot dogs on starchy buns, use romaine lettuce leaves! Kids love this for a quick and healthy after-school snack!

Lettuce Leaf Hot Dogs

INGREDIENTS

1   package turkey hot dogs

1 or 2 Taylor Farms Romaine Hearts (separated, rinsed, and dried)

Prepared yellow mustard

Makes 8 sandwiches

INSTRUCTIONS

Cook hot dogs according to package directions.

Place each hot dog in the center of a lettuce leaf and top with mustard. Serve with a helping of sugar snap peas instead of french fries or potato chips!

By using a lettuce leaf instead of a bun, you save about 100 calories per sandwich.

Burgers are a must for family meals, and this burger recipe has it all! Lower in fat, super low in calories, great tasting, and really easy to make!

Taylor Farms Turkey Lettuce Burgers

INGREDIENTS

2 pounds ground turkey

1 envelope dry onion soup mix

½ cup prepared BBQ sauce

2 heads Taylor Farms Iceberg Lettuce (rinsed, dried, and leaves separated)

Cooking spray

Optional garnishes:
Sliced tomatoes, sliced avocado, pickles, mustard, catsup

Makes 8 burgers

INSTRUCTIONS

In a mixing bowl, combine turkey, onion soup mix, and BBQ sauce; mix well.

Form eight patties. The thinner the patties, the quicker they will cook.

Spray non-stick cooking spray on indoor or outdoor grill. Grill burgers over medium-high heat until meat is no longer pink.

Place each burger on one lettuce leaf and add all your favorite garnishes. Finish with another lettuce leaf on top. Serve warm.

Large hamburger buns can have over 200 calories per bun, while iceberg lettuce leaves have less than 5 calories per leaf!

SALINAS VALLEY MEMORIAL HEALTHCARE SYSTEM

I create healthy lunch ideas for Salinas Valley Memorial Healthcare System's Asthma Camp.

I come up with innovative healthy food ideas that kids love, and conduct food demonstrations using a lot of fresh veggies. Kids are excited to take these simple cooking concepts back to their families and show their parents how they can easily increase their intake of fresh fruits and vegetables and help their families maintain a healthier lifestyle.

Salinas Valley Memorial Healthcare System is a leader in community healthcare outreach. I have been involved in their "Ask the Expert" outreach program for Cardiac, Diabetes, Joint Replacement, and Cancer Treatment. I also enjoy conducting healthy eating demonstrations for the healthcare providers of SVMH. It's a great opportunity for me to serve up yummy helpings of fresh produce in an educational, yet entertaining way.

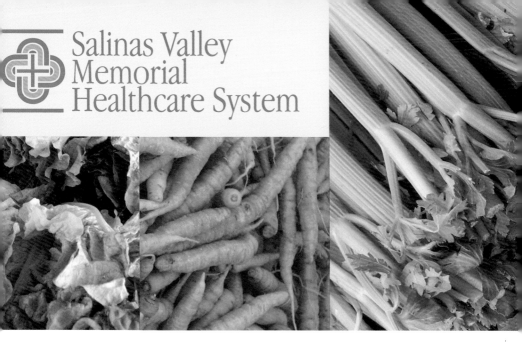

Salinas Valley Memorial Healthcare System is dedicated to improving the health and well being of the people in the Central Coast region of California. Through the decades, Salinas Valley Memorial has demonstrated a commitment to excellence, bringing expert, technologically advanced care to local communities. Today, the hospital's services reach beyond the main campus into neighborhoods throughout the Central Coast region offering the highest quality healthcare services for people who are ill or injured and helping people live healthier lives through prevention and education efforts.

www.svmh.com

This recipe concept encourages us to drink more water and enjoy the taste in the process! And these water tea bottles have zero calories and no artificial sweeteners! A super cost-effective way to keep hydrated and healthy!

Tea Water Bottles

INGREDIENTS

12 16.9 fluid-ounce water bottles

12 herbal flavored tea bags

Note: I like to use green tea for adults and fruit flavored herbal teas for children: berry, orange, pomegranate, and lemon.

Makes 12 bottles of tea

INSTRUCTIONS

Remove the caps from 12 water bottles and pour out about 1 tablespoon of water from each bottle. Fold the dry tea bags in half and insert one tea bag into each water bottle. Recap the bottles and place them in the refrigerator overnight to steep.

Remove the tea bags the next morning. Enjoy the bottles of tea water chilled, or freeze the bottles of tea water and thaw in lunch bags for an icy cold beverage at lunchtime!

I also like to serve tea water over ice with a fresh squeeze of lemon, lime, tangerine, or orange. Healthy never tasted so good. It's also so inexpensive!

During summer months, place a frozen tea water bottle in your lunch. It will keep your sandwich cool and become a refreshing lunchtime drink!

This recipe raises eyebrows! I use a lemon cake mix and replace the oil that the packaged directions call for with one cup of mashed, cooked cauliflower. I also add one cup of toasted coconut for a wonderful flavor! The result is a tasty cake that is on the "most requested" list! I even use these little cakes as a base for mini shortcakes.

Lemon Cauliflower Cupcakes

INGREDIENTS

1 18-oz packaged lemon cake mix

3 egg whites or **2** whole eggs

1 cup cooked mashed cauliflower (cooled)

1 cup water

1 cup toasted coconut

Optional: 1 cup white chocolate chips

Makes 24 cupcakes or 48 mini cupcakes

INSTRUCTIONS

Preheat oven to 350°.

In a large mixing bowl of an electric mixer, add the dry cake mix and other ingredients and mix on low speed for one minute. Scrape bowl and continue to mix at medium-high speed for 4 minutes until batter is well combined.

Line muffin tins with 24 cupcake papers.

Use an ice-cream scoop to fill papers a little more than half full with batter. Place tins in preheated oven and bake for 20 to 25 minutes until cake springs back when lightly touched.

Remove cupcakes from oven and place on a cooling rack. Dust cooled cupcakes with a light dusting of powdered sugar, or frost with a non-dairy whipped topping.

Store frosted cupcakes in the refrigerator until ready to eat.

Mini cupcakes are perfect for school parties and special events!

Salads are a great choice, but salad dressings can really pack on the calories. Try this easy creamy dressing that cuts calories in half!

Creamy Salsa Dressing

INGREDIENTS

½ cup bottled salsa or fresh pico de gallo

2 Tbsp. fat-free ranch-style salad dressing

Makes about ½ cup of dressing

INSTRUCTIONS

In a small bowl, mix salsa and dressing together. Toss with your favorite salad or spoon over lettuce wedges.

Refrigerate any leftover dressing in an airtight container.

Most salsas are only 10 calories for 2 tablespoons, whereas typical ranch-style dressing has 140 calories for 2 tablespoons!

Corn on the cob, a food that just screams summer, is a healthy choice, but slathering on butter or even butter substitutes can really pack on the calories and fat. This fun and easy recipe is a great way to get your family to enjoy sweet fresh corn without all the extra fat!

BBQ Corn on the Cob

INGREDIENTS

6 corn on the cob (husked or with husks on)

6 Tbsp. prepared BBQ sauce

Makes 6 cobs

INSTRUCTIONS

Heat outdoor or indoor grill to medium-high heat.

Husks on: Before grilling, fold down husks and remove corn silks, and then brush BBQ sauce on the cobs and fold husks back around the corn.

Husked: Place husked corn cobs directly on the grill and brush each one with 1 tablespoon of BBQ sauce.

Grill corn and turn often until BBQ sauce caramelizes and corn is hot (about 6 minutes.) Serve immediately and enjoy!

Note: You can also substitute dry BBQ seasoning for BBQ sauce. Just spray each cob with cooking spray and lightly sprinkle with dry mesquite or BBQ seasoning. Grill as directed above.

Two tablespoons of butter is 200 calories, whereas two tablespoons of prepared BBQ sauce is only 14 calories!

I serve this delicious cole slaw at family functions, and it's always a popular side dish at barbecues.

American Apple Cole Slaw

INGREDIENTS

2 apples (rinsed, dried, cored, and diced)

1 cup dried cranberries

8 cups green cabbage (finely chopped)

3 cups purple cabbage (finely chopped)

2 carrots (grated)

1 cup fat-free whipped dressing (mayonnaise substitute)

2 Tbsp. fresh lemon juice

2 Tbsp. apple cider vinegar or white wine vinegar

2 Tbsp. honey or sugar

½ tsp. salt

Pepper to taste

Makes 12 cups of salad

INSTRUCTIONS

In a large bowl, mix whipped dressing, vinegar, honey, and lemon juice. Add apples, cranberries, green cabbage, purple cabbage, carrots, and salt and pepper. Toss until well combined. Refrigerate until ready to serve.

SVMH takes pride in offering healthy recipes to the community and this cole slaw is a wonderful example.

HEALTHY EATING LIFESTYLE PRINCIPLES

The HELP organization is very dear to my heart. I was involved with this wonderful nonprofit organization since it began, and I have grown right along with it. Connecting with kids through the preparation of healthy foods is a reward that is unmatched, and I have made many friends for life by being connected to this fruitful organization.

HELP's mission is in complete alignment with the First Lady's "Let's Move" campaign. One of the many movements HELP supports is to provide fresh salad bars in school lunchrooms!

I was honored to represent the HELP organization at the White House for the kickoff of the "Chefs Move to Schools" campaign. And because of that experience, I made a personal commitment to the First Lady to educate our families and children through hands-on cooking classes, retreats, and the recipes in this cookbook.

Thank you HELP for leading the way to a healthier and happier life for so many children and families!

Healthy Eating Lifestyle Principles, Inc. (HELP) is a non-profit agency whose mission is to promote healthy eating, physical activity, and the increased consumption of fresh fruits and vegetables among youth and adults. HELP encourages healthy living by offering nutrition education and physical activity to the community of Monterey County by teaching students and adults how to make healthy food choices.

HELP was founded in June 2004 by community leader Basil Mills as a special agriculture-based initiative of the Monterey County Office of Economic Development and Monterey County Business Council with the support of the Grower-Shipper Association Foundation.

www.helpchooseyourlife.org

HELP's Junior Chefs,
Katelyn Hoffman &
Kody Hoffman

These individual pizzas are easy for the kids to make and easy for you to bake. They taste great out of the oven or straight off the outdoor grill!

Whole-Wheat Pita Pizza

INGREDIENTS

4 whole-wheat pitas

8 Tbsp. marinara sauce or pasta sauce

4 slices turkey ham (cut into strips)

8 tsp. grated Parmesan cheese

Dried oregano or Italian seasoning for sprinkling on tops of pizzas

Makes 4 pizzas

INSTRUCTIONS

Heat oven or covered outdoor grill to 425°.

On each pita, spread 2 tablespoons of the marinara sauce.

Top each pizza with strips of turkey ham.

Sprinkle each pizza with 2 teaspoons of Parmesan cheese, and top with a sprinkle of dried oregano or Italian seasoning.

Place pizza directly on oven rack or outdoor grill and bake for 10 to 15 minutes or until pita is hot and crispy. Cut each pizza into quarters and enjoy!

Use grated Parmesan cheese instead of mozzarella cheese—2 teaspoons of Parmesan is only 20 calories!

One cup of cucumber slices is only 16 calories!

Cucumber Crackers

INGREDIENTS

1 large fresh cucumber (rinsed, dried, and cut into 12 to 15 rounds)

½ cup organic peanut butter

Makes 12 to 15 cucumber snacks

INSTRUCTIONS

With a butter knife, spread peanut butter on each cucumber round. Serve immediately for a healthy snack.

You can make these snacks ahead of time and store on a plate covered with plastic food wrap in the refrigerator until you are ready to eat them.

> *Instead of serving high-fat crackers for a snack, try sliced cucumbers with a variety of toppings. Cucumbers are super low in calories and they really satisfy with the crunch that we like our snack foods to have!*

Fruit can make any salad more exciting! Use the flavor combinations to create guilt-free delicious salads.

Add Fruit to Your Salad Bar

FLAVORFUL COMBINATIONS

8 cups Fresh Baby Spinach and
2 cups Watermelon Cubes
(crumbled feta cheese is optional)

---

8 cups green leaf lettuce and
2 cups tangerine segments

---

8 cups chopped Romaine Hearts and
2 cups Cantaloupe Cubes (fresh grated
Parmesan Cheese is optional)

---

8 cups Mixed Baby Greens and
2 cups Seedless Grapes
(crumbled Blue Cheese is optional)

8 cups shredded Green Cabbage and
2 cups Pineapple Chunks

---

8 cups Butter Lettuce and
2 cups Honey Dew Melon (Fresh grated
Parmesan Cheese is optional)

---

8 cups baby Romaine mix and
2 cups Fresh Peaches and Blueberries

---

8 cups Green Leaf Lettuce and
2 cups Fresh sliced Kiwi Fruit

Add **2** cups cooked and cubed boneless-skinless chicken or turkey breast to any of the above salad combinations for a healthy, complete meal.

Each salad serves 4

FRUIT JUICE SALAD DRESSING

⅛ cup extra virgin olive oil
¼ cup fruit juice (orange, tangerine, apple, cranberry, or pomegranate)
Pinch of salt and pepper

1 Tbsp. fresh finely chopped herbs
   (basil, rosemary, mint, tarragon, or oregano)
2 Tbsp. vinegar (balsamic, apple cider vinegar, red wine vinegar, etc.)

INSTRUCTIONS

In a small bowl, whisk the selected ingredients together and toss with your favorite fruit and fresh green salad. Serve immediately.

TIP: Fresh rosemary and oregano is one of my favorite combinations!

Breakfast was never so tasty and fun! Make plenty of parfaits, because you will want one too!

Summertime Strawberry Parfaits

INGREDIENTS

1 basket of fresh strawberries (rinsed, blotted dry, and sliced)

4 6-ounce containers low-fat or fat-free vanilla yogurt

4 tsp. of whole-grain cereal

Makes 4 parfaits

INSTRUCTIONS

Place a layer of sliced fresh strawberries at the bottom of each plastic cup or parfait glass.

Spoon half the yogurt over the strawberries and then repeat the layers of strawberries and yogurt, reserving some yogurt as a final topping.

Top the strawberries with remaining yogurt and sprinkle with cereal. Cover each glass with plastic food wrap and store in the refrigerator until ready to serve.

These parfaits also make great birthday treats to take to school instead of store-bought cupcakes or other high-fat snacks.

Pineapple Ice Pops

INGREDIENTS

1 fresh pineapple (cored, peeled, and cut into 2-inch spears)

Lollipop sticks or wooden craft sticks

Makes 8 to 10 pops

INSTRUCTIONS

Insert a stick into the end of each pineapple spear and place on a cookie sheet lined with foil. Cover the spears with a sheet of foil and freeze overnight. Place the frozen spears in a gallon freezer bag and seal. Return to the freezer and store until ready to eat.

These naturally sweet pops are a full serving of fruit with no added sugar.

You will use this recipe over and over again! One package of cake mix and a cup of cooked veggies make this quick homemade cookie a family favorite!

Cake Mix Surprise Drop Cookies

INGREDIENTS

1 packaged cake mix (chocolate, white, spice, yellow, carrot, or lemon)

2 whole eggs

1 cup of well-cooked vegetables, mashed or finely chopped (butternut squash, broccoli cole slaw, sweet potato, pumpkin or cauliflower).

2 cups oatmeal

1 cup optional stir-ins: raisins, chopped nuts, chocolate chips, butterscotch chips, peanut butter chips, white chocolate chips, toasted coconut, or dried cranberries.

Makes about 2½ dozen cookies

INSTRUCTIONS

Preheat oven to 350°.

Cook and cool the vegetables.

With an electric mixer (with paddle attachment), mix together cake mix, eggs, oatmeal, and cooked cooled vegetables until well combined. Add optional stir-ins. (If dough is dry and does not hold together, add one more egg.)

Form dough into balls (a mini ice-cream scoop works great) and place two inches apart on a prepared cookie sheet. Bake for 5 minutes, and then lightly mash cookies down with the back of a cookie spatula (spray a little cooking spray on spatula to avoid sticking). Continue to bake cookies for another 5 to 8 minutes until they appear set and dry.

Remove the cookie sheet from the oven, and use a spatula to transfer the cookies to a cooling rack.

Store the cookies in an airtight container in the refrigerator for up to five days.

Try these combinations:

- *Lemon cake mix, cauliflower, toasted coconut, and white chocolate chips*
- *Yellow cake mix, sweet potato, and peanut butter chips*
- *Spice cake mix, butternut squash, chopped pecans, and raisins*
- *Chocolate cake mix, broccoli cole slaw, and chocolate chips*
- *Carrot cake mix, sweet potato, walnuts, and butterscotch chips*

DRUMMOND CULINARY ACADEMY AT RANCHO CIELO

Sometimes words are not enough to describe an experience that changes one's life, and that is how I feel about the students at the Drummond Culinary Academy at Rancho Cielo in Salinas, California.

From the first time I set foot on this exceptional campus, I felt I belonged. Many of the students at the Drummond Academy are striving to discover their true talents and passions in life and use those talents to make the world a better place. I, too, have taken this journey, just a little later in life. Unlocking one's true passion is a gift that these students are receiving, and I am honored to be a small part of their amazing transformations.

Whenever I need inspiration in my own life, I drive to the Rancho Cielo campus. My admiration for the students and all the folks that are instrumental in keeping this program going overwhelms me with a sense that this is really the way community is supposed to be.

DRUMMOND CULINARY ACADEMY

The Rancho Cielo Drummond Culinary Academy in Salinas, California, is dedicated to providing at-risk youth an opportunity to gain classroom training, work experience, and transferable skills that help them become employable in the culinary and hospitality industry. Through its partnership with the John Muir Charter School, students achieve their high school diploma; the rest of their studies take place in the commercial kitchen with a Certified Executive Chef, working through the National Restaurant Association's Pro Start curriculum. The students learn both through the curriculum as well as by serving diners when the Academy Dining Room is open weekly to the public.

Visit *www.ranchocieloyc.org* for more information about the school and dining reservations.

Whether it's chili for a big game or an outdoor barbecue, this recipe has it all—great taste, easy to make, and nutritious!

"The name speaks for itself. I can't wait until I make this healthy version of chili for my grandmother. I am going to make it for our next family gathering!"

Anthony Michael Turpin-Guzman
Rancho Cielo Culinary Student

The Best Chili Ever

INGREDIENTS

- **1** red bell pepper (diced)
- **1** green bell pepper (diced)
- **1** yellow onion (diced)
- **1** 12-ounce bag Mann's Broccoli Cole Slaw (cooked in the microwave for 5 minutes, cooled, and chopped)
- **2** pounds ground turkey
- **2** tsp. garlic salt
- **1** Tbsp. chili powder
- **2** tsp. ground allspice

Makes 15 to 20 servings

- **2** Tbsp. ground cumin
- **3** 15-ounce cans chili beans (with liquid)
- **1** 15-ounce can garbanzo beans (drained)
- **2** 15-ounce cans red kidney beans (drained)
- **3** 15-ounce cans pinto beans (with liquid)
- **2** cups prepared mild salsa
- **1½** cups prepared BBQ sauce
- **2** Tbsp. olive oil

INSTRUCTIONS

In a large pot over medium-high heat, add olive oil and the red and green bell peppers and onion. Sauté until vegetables are very tender. Add turkey, cooked broccoli coleslaw, and spices to peppers and onion mixture, and cook until the meat is no longer pink.

Add the canned beans, salsa, and BBQ sauce to the meat mixture. Mix all the ingredients together over medium-high heat until the beans are heated through. Reduce heat and simmer chili for 15 minutes. Serve in bowls.

You can transfer the cooked chili to a slowcooker to keep it warm for a perfect buffet dish!

This is the first recipe that I learned to make when I was taking culinary classes in Italy. This salt is used in soups, sauces, meats, and stews. I make a large quantity at a time and store it in glass jars. It is a staple in my everyday cooking!

"The Aromatic salt is an awesome idea to include on the spice shelf. I look forward to creating my own blend!"

Chantel Amaro
Rancho Cielo Culinary Student

Aromatic Salt

INGREDIENTS

3 cups coarse sea salt

2 3-inch branches fresh rosemary (rosemary needles stripped off rosemary stems)

8 large sage leaves or 16 small leaves

6 whole cloves of garlic (peeled)

1½ tsp. dried red pepper flakes (the type used on pizza)

Makes 3 cups

INSTRUCTIONS

Strip leaves off rosemary and sage stems. Place all ingredients in a food processor and grind together until well combined. This will take just a few seconds.

Store aromatic salt in glass jars, but for the first 24 to 48 hours after salt is made, keep the lids off the jars so the salt has a chance to dry out. The herbs will make the salt look very green at first, until they have dried in the salt mixture. After 24 to 48 hours, place lids on jars.

Aromatic Salt is a wonderful gift from the kitchen—perfect for a hostess gift!

I learned to make this wonderfully simple sauce in a small medieval town in Tuscany, Italy. I am thrilled that the students of the Drummond Culinary Academy at Rancho Cielo are making this sauce, too.

"This recipe was fun to make, and the sauce tastes better than what most restaurants make. The recipe takes the saying 'Home is where the heart is' to the next level!"

Cassandra Adkins
Rancho Cielo Culinary Student

Authentic Tuscan Tomato Sauce

INGREDIENTS

3 medium purple onions

6 cloves of garlic

3 small carrots

3 stalks of celery

1 large bunch of fresh basil (chopped)

3 1 pound 12 ounce cans of imported canned tomatoes (from Italy)

3 Tbsp. olive oil

Aromatic salt (recipe on page 151)

Pepper to taste

Makes about 12 cups of sauce

INSTRUCTIONS

Coarsely chop onion, carrots, celery, and garlic. In a large Dutch oven or soup pot, add olive oil to cover the bottom of the pan and cook chopped vegetables over medium-high heat. Cook veggies until they are tender, stirring with a wooden spoon.

Add tomatoes, chopped basil, and salt and pepper to taste. Stir briefly and cover with lid. After sauce starts to boil, reduce the heat and let sauce simmer slowly for about one hour. Stir the sauce every now and then to prevent it from sticking to the bottom of the pot. Remove sauce from heat. Using a hand blender, blend sauce until creamy. Store cooled sauce in the refrigerator or the freezer.

Use this sauce on pizza; over pasta, chicken, eggplant, or zucchini; or as a soup base!

This recipe was a happy mistake! I left my broccoli cole slaw meatballs in the oven way too long, which really dried them out. Instead of throwing away food, I decided to add the meatballs to a brothy soup and see if they would get tender again. I was pleasantly surprised that not only did the meatballs soften up and take on the flavors of this tasty broth, my husband loved the soup!

Albondigas Soup (Meatball Soup)

INGREDIENTS

2	Tbsp. olive oil
½	cup red bell pepper (chopped)
1	large purple onion (chopped)
3	stalks of celery (roughly chopped)
5	carrots (roughly chopped)
6	red potatoes (peeled and quartered)
5	cloves of garlic (finely chopped)
1	tsp. cumin seed (crushed)
1	tsp. garlic salt
½	cup cilantro (chopped)
10	cups prepared beef broth
2	bay leaves
½	head of green cabbage (cut into large chunks)
24	baked Broccoli Cole Slaw Meatballs (recipe on page 33)

Serves 8 to10

INSTRUCTIONS

In a large soup pot over medium-high heat, add olive oil, red pepper, and onion. Sauté until the onions and peppers are tender. Add all other ingredients and bring the soup to a boil. Reduce heat and simmer for 40 to 50 minutes until vegetables are very tender and potatoes, cabbage, and carrots are well cooked.

> *This recipe has a twist for an interesting take on the traditional Mexican Albondigas Soup!*

It's a fun and creative salad that looks delish! You can even serve the salad in lettuce leaves for Cinco de Mayo wraps!

Desiree Cabrera
Rancho Cielo Culinary Student

Cinco de Mayo Salad

SALAD INGREDIENTS

2 12-ounce bags of Broccoli Cole Slaw

1 15-ounce can of black beans (drained and rinsed)

1   bunch cilantro (chopped)

1 cup frozen petite corn (white or yellow)

1 bunch green onions (chopped)

2 cups grape tomatoes (rinsed, dried, and sliced)

2 cups chopped, cooked boneless-skinless chicken breast (12 to 16 ounce)

1 Tbsp. mesquite seasoning (optional)

2 tsp. ground cumin

3 Tbsp. fresh lime juice

½ tsp. garlic salt

Optional garnish: lime slices and sprigs of fresh cilantro

Serves 8 to 10

DRESSING INGREDIENTS

½ cup low-calorie ranch-style dressing

½ cup mild salsa

¼ cup BBQ sauce

INSTRUCTIONS

In a large mixing bowl, combine all of the salad ingredients and toss.

In a small mixing bowl, add all the dressing ingredients and whisk together until well combined.

Drizzle dressing over salad and toss until well mixed.

Plate salad on a large serving platter and garnish with sliced limes and cilantro sprigs.

> *Sometimes when I cook a Mexican meal, I realize that the recipe does not include enough fresh vegetables. This Mexican-inspired dish includes a bushel of freshness that makes it delicious!*

This refreshing frozen dessert takes only minutes to prepare! The students at Rancho Cielo suggest that you use this as an impressive "intermezzo" for a multicourse dinner!

"This is Happy Food!"

Anthony Michael Turpin-Guzman
Rancho Cielo Culinary Student

The Best Fresh Lemon Frozen Yogurt

INGREDIENTS

4 cups non-fat vanilla yogurt

6 Tbsp. fresh lemon juice (Meyer lemons are best for juicing)

1 tsp. grated lemon peel

¾ cup sugar

Optional garnish: sprig of fresh lavender

Makes one quart

INSTRUCTIONS

Beat together the yogurt, lemon juice, lemon peel, and sugar in a bowl of an electric mixer for about 2 minutes, until the sugar is dissolved.

Pour the mixture into a tabletop ice-cream maker (pre-frozen ice-cream drum.) Turn the ice-cream machine on and churn for about 30 minutes, until the yogurt is very thick. Store the frozen yogurt in a covered, airtight container until ready to serve.

I like to serve this yogurt in a hollowed-out lemon. Simply cut a lemon in half and scoop out the pulp. Freeze lemon shells on a baking sheet and fill each with a small scoop of frozen yogurt when ready to serve. Place filled lemon cups in pretty stemmed sherbet or champagne glasses. Garnish frozen yogurt with lemon zest. Add a sprig of fresh lavender if desired.

Chef Paola, Italy

ACKNOWLEDGEMENTS

This cookbook is the result of the many wonderful people and organizations that planted seeds of encouragement in my life and in the lives of children and families that want healthier lifestyles.

First, to the growers who are profiled in this book, I cannot say thank you enough. Farmers are the hardest working people I know, and the growers I've written about have dedicated their lives to bringing top quality fruits and vegetables to our tables.

Next, to the community organizations that care for our children, most notably Rancho Cielo Youth Campus and all the people who made this miraculous school come to life, you are a model for what the world should be. Salinas Valley Memorial Healthcare System and to the HELP organization (Healthy Eating Lifestyle Principles), I thank you for your dedication to the well-being of children and families through education and the promotion of healthy eating. Your commitment to the community is so honorable.

And this book would not have happened without "The Team" that appeared out of nowhere! Olivia Trinidad, Lisa Mathews, Carrie Gwynne, Lisa Vradenburg, Brenda Rysdam, and Sherry Cross—what in the world would I have done without your talents, dedication,

and love for what you do best. I am forever grateful to my "top shelf" team of women and friends who helped bring this book into the hands of families all over the world.

To my family, the ones I have been cooking for all my life: My husband Mark; my daughters Jill, Shannon, and Heidi Miller; my son-in-laws Daniel and Jim; my grandkids Madison, Spencer (my grandson-chef in the making), Baylee, Eden, and my dear boys Gavin, and Dylan, and the baby on-the-way. To my brother Greg and wife Toni #1, my brother Jamie and Toni # 2, my nieces and nephews Kevin, Matthew, Sarah, Elena, Jamie Lou, Elyssa, and Emily. Throughout the years, you all have expressed your love for me by sitting at my table, and that has been the most valuable encouragement that I could ever ask for.

To my Italian cooking instructor and friend Paola Baccetti from Casa Ombuto in Poppi, Italy, your life has been an inspiration to me and I am grateful for your passion for food. We are sisters for life!

Thank you to Michelle Obama, our First Lady of the United States, for igniting the spark within me through your "Chefs Move to Schools" campaign. Your gracious invitation to the White House changed my life.

And with deep appreciation to all of the hundreds of men, women, and children who stood at my cooking demos and inspired me to write this book, thank you.